HOW TO SHOOT
A HANDGUN:
*Handgun Marksmanship
Fundamentals for Real Life Situations*

including specific information will be considered an illegal act irrespective of if it is done electronically or in print. This extends to creating a secondary or tertiary copy of the work or a recorded copy and is only allowed with express written consent from the Publisher. All additional right reserved.

The information in the following pages is broadly considered to be a truthful and accurate account of facts and as such any inattention, use or misuse of the information in question by the reader will render any resulting actions solely under their purview. There are no scenarios in which the publisher or the original author of this work can be in any fashion deemed liable for any hardship or damages that may befall them after undertaking information described herein.

Additionally, the information in the following pages is intended only for informational purposes and should thus be thought of as universal. As befitting its nature, it is presented without assurance regarding its prolonged validity or interim quality. Trademarks that are mentioned are done without written consent and can in no way be considered an endorsement from the trademark holder.

Table of Contents

INTRODUCTION

Congratulations on downloading *How to Shoot a Handgun: Handgun Marksmanship Fundamentals for Real Life Situations* and thank you for doing so. So, you have made the decision to purchase a gun for self-protection. Congratulations! However, if you are like many new would-be marksmen, you aren't quite sure what to do next and, more importantly, how to practice with your weapon and shoot it safely.

Luckily, the following chapters will discuss everything you need to know in order to not only shoot a pistol effectively when you are practicing on a range, but also everything you need to know in order to use your new weapon for self-defense should the need arise. First and foremost, you will learn all about the mindset required for self-defense including the importance of total situational awareness and the levels of readiness that you will need to master in order to keep yourself and your loved ones' safe at all times and in all situations. Next, you will learn all about the various components of your handgun, what they do and why they are important.

From there you will learn about various types of hand positions as well as trigger management to ensure your aim is as accurate as possible. Then you will learn about proper stances to take while shooting and why they are the foundation of all well-placed shots. From there you will learn how to draw your gun from its holster effectively and also how to reload efficiently to ensure you know what to do in case you find yourself in a real-life scenario where such things could save your life. With that out of the way, you will learn how to recognize common handgun malfunctions as well as how to repair them in the safest way possible.

Moving on, you will learn how to deal with multiple or moving targets effectively and how to practice for real-world scenarios where you find yourself outnumbered. With that completed, you will then learn several practical drills to help improve the key aspects of perfect marksmanship. Finally, you will learn several different alternative shooting techniques so you are never without recourse even if the situation doesn't favor standard shooting conditions.

There are plenty of books on this subject on the market, thanks again for choosing this one! Every effort was made to ensure it is full of as much useful information as possible, please enjoy!

CHAPTER 1
Mindset of Marksmanship for Self-Defense

W hen it comes to self-defense, there are a few different mindsets. While a combat mindset may suit those who expect to, or actively seek out, combat on a regular basis, self-defense requires a different mindset entirely. Basically, it boils down to two things, you need to be willing to do what it takes in order to protect yourself and your family which means you need to prioritize not being hurt and not being defeated. You will need to maintain the ability to act both effectively and, more importantly, morally while under emotional and possibly

11

physical stress. The proper mindset will focus on not just what is legal but what is moral in a specific situation.

Last resort: In general, you are going to only want to fire your weapon when the actions your enemy is taking are so terrible that you are willing to stop them regardless of the consequences. If you hope to mortally wound someone then that action must not be hindered by moral or legal boundaries. This is an extremely high standard, and for good reason, you will not be able to maintain a defensive mindset unless you develop both self-control and the ability to accurately judge situations while under pressure. With the proper mindset, fear is mitigated and anger is pushed out of the equation entirely.

A prerequisite of the self-defense mindset is confidence in your abilities to the point that you won't second-guess yourself when the time comes to put your training to use. Only by being completely aware of your own strengths and weaknesses will you be able to act appropriately when confronted by a real threat. If you are not completely aware of your own limitations, then when this type of situation arises you have a greater chance of panicking or otherwise acting inappropriately.

Additionally, you will want to keep in mind that a firearm is not there to prevent small physical scuffles or to help you enforce your will on others, it is there for one reason and one reason only, to save lives when it matters most. When the time comes to use it for its intended purpose, it is important to take into account the moral and ethical questions that are required and know that you are making the right choice with complete certainty. If you don't operate with absolute certainty in this instance then you may hesitate and get yourself killed or you may kill or maim someone who doesn't truly deserve it. Whatever the situation forces you to do, you will want to first ensure that you and your loved ones will be able to easily live with the consequences of your actions after the fact.

Total situational awareness

A crucial part of having an effective personal defense mindset is total situational awareness. This means you are always going to want to be fully aware of your surroundings instead of walking through life oblivious to the potential dangers that surround you. This means more than avoiding open manhole covers or freshly waxed floors, it means being aware of the people around you who may have the inclination to do you harm. Clarity of thought is extremely important to total situational awareness and can potentially save you from harm even if you are not currently armed. If you mind is unfocused and cluttered then the added stress of an attack can cause you to go into sensory overload. If this occurs then everything you may have learned or practiced for can easily be forgotten in a split second. A key part of keeping a personal defense mindset is being able to instantly make the decision to defend yourself when it is required.

While there is nothing wrong with preferring not to fight as a general rule, that mindset must necessarily go out the window if you hope to defend yourself and your loved ones from an attack. If you would rather lay down your own life then harm someone else, that is your choice, but your family might have other ideas. Without total situational awareness, it can be easy to lose the clarity of purpose you need to attack in the moment as you may regret or second guess your actions. If this is the case then self-defense is not truly possible in the moment and you may live to regret your decision later, if you are lucky.

In order to enhance your total situational awareness skills, keep the following in mind:

Don't look like prey: First and foremost, if you don't look like you would be an easy target then you are less likely to be considered a target. This means you are going to want to keep your heads up and your eyes scanning your surroundings. Studies show that something as simple as sustained eye contact can decrease your odds of being considered a target by more than 50 percent. You will also want to walk with purpose with your shoulders squared and your head held high. Don't look like a weak member of the herd and you won't be treated like one.

Keep distractions to a minimum: Avoid letting technology or window-shopping shift your focus completely from your surroundings. Additionally, your ability to process visual stimuli will decrease if you are listening to music. This is why smartphone users make such prime targets. Keep distractions to a minimum and stay alert.

Be aware of your priority awareness zone: Try and keep an eye on everything that is happening within 15-yards of your current location at all time. Take time to look behind you now and then and keep an eye on anyone who enters this radius. Start close to your location and work outwards. Additionally, you will want to be aware of things in your vicinity that can be used to aid in your defense. Finally, always be aware of specific escape routes.

Readiness conditions

The combat mindset uses colors to denote various levels of readiness, these colors have been adapted here to outline the conditions for the personal defense mindset.

White condition: This condition is akin to being completely unaware of what is going on around you. In the white condition, you are only aware of your position and are otherwise completely consumed with what you are doing or are so relaxed that nothing else seems to matter. In this condition, it is unlikely that you would notice a threat until it is too late to do anything about it. Predators tend to thrive on individuals who are in the white condition as they are the easiest to overpower and thus make the most promising targets. Ideally you will only allow yourself the luxury of this condition if you are sleeping somewhere safe or in your home behind locked doors.

Yellow condition: This condition should be your default condition whenever you are out in the world where a threat could conceivably come upon you at practically any time. While it may not be possible for you to maintain this level of awareness at all times at first, it will become easier with practice. The basics of this condition include being alert for specific threats in your surroundings even though no attack is obviously incoming. In this condition, you will be ready to move into action as soon as you notice anything that could lead to a threat. In general, you are keeping an eye on the details of the world around you.

Orange condition: You should enter this condition once you have identified a potential threat while already in condition yellow. What you have identified doesn't necessarily need to actually be a threat, but the potential of a threatening scenario should be enough to put you into a relatively high alert. The first response in these scenarios should always be to try and avoid escalating the situation by either leaving the zone of the potential threat or contacting the proper authorities. This condition doesn't necessarily mean you have come into contact with a human threat, it could also be things like a dark alley that you have accidentally wandered into, returning home to a broken window or open door or a drunk individual who looks as though they are itching for a fight.

Red condition: You will want to escalate to this condition if a confrontation or dangerous situation seems essentially unavoidable and defensive action is most likely going to be required. In this condition, you will have identified a real threat that is currently approaching you in a serious and combative manner. You should be able to tell beyond a shadow of a doubt that their attention is focused on you and that they have a clear intention of doing you harm. Essentially at this point you are all but in the middle of a fight that is waiting to happen.

CHAPTER 2
Handgun Components

Handguns come in a wide variety of shapes and sizes that are well suited to a variety of tasks. Generally, they all have the same basic components, however, which are described in detail below.

Core handgun components

All types of handguns have a few components in common.

Frame: The frame constitutes the core structure of the pistol to which all the other various pieces are attached.

21

Barrel: The barrel is the hollow tube on the front of the gun through which bullet ultimately travels once the gun has been fired. The inside of the barrel is grooved, which is known as rifled, in order to help the bullet to spin and improve both accuracy and velocity. Velocity is also controlled by the length of the barrel with shorter barrels providing less velocity than longer barrels.

Trigger: The trigger is the release device of the interconnected firing system that makes handguns such an effective weapon. It is typically a curved piece of metal that is activated through pressure from the user's finger which activates the hammer and starts the firing process.

Trigger guard: The trigger guard is a piece of metal that surrounds the trigger for the purpose of preventing misfires.

Hammer: The hammer is another part of the firing system. It is attached to the trigger but is located at the back of the gun. When the trigger is pulled the hammer moves back and then springs forward with enough force to set the firing process in motion. The hammer connects with the firing pin to ignite gunpowder and cause the bullet to fire.

Firing pin: The firing pin is located behind the primer of a fresh cartridge, once it is struck by the hammer it moves rapidly forward, connecting with the primer cap and causing the gun to fire.

Muzzle: The muzzle of a gun is the front portion of the barrel when the projectile exits the gun.

Grip: The portion of the gun that you hold onto is referred to as the grip.

Handgun categories

All handguns can be split into three main categories, machine pistols, semiautomatic pistols and revolvers.

Revolver: A revolver is a type of repeating handgun that has, as the name implies, a revolving cylinder that is filled with individual chambers. While the term revolver is typically used in association with handguns, handguns aren't the only type of gun with revolving chambers. Typically, a revolver will contain either five or six chambers. The revolver is useful as it allows the user to fire several rounds in a row without having to reload in any capacity. Every time the hammer is cocked, the cylinder revolves to align the next chamber which is where the gun gets its name. If the revolver is single-action then the user pulls the hammer back with one hand and the trigger is used to fire the gun. If it is a double action revolver then pulling the trigger also moves the hammer back prior to firing which requires more tension on the trigger to get the job done. Loading is accomplished via opening the cylinder and manually reloading the bullets.

Semiautomatic pistol: A semiautomatic is any pistol that utilizes the energy of the previously fired cartridge to cycle the action of the firearm with the purpose of moving the next cartridge into position for firing. One cartridge will be fired each time the trigger is pulled. The disconnector is the part of the pistol that ensures this is the case. The semiautomatic pistol is likely the most common type of pistol that you will encounter. Synonyms for the semiautomatic pistol include the self-loading pistol, autoloading pistol and autopistol.

A semiautomatic pistol utilizes the energy from the previous shot to reload the chamber for the next shot. Once the proceeding round is fired, the casing is ejected from the gun and the next round it moved into the chamber. The most typical way for this to occur is through recoil operation though gas operation and blowback are also used. A majority of semiautomatic pistols are loaded with removable magazines that store the ammunition in the grip of the gun.

The semiautomatic and the machine pistol also have a few extra components compared to the standard revolver. The slide is the steel upper portion of a semiautomatic or machine pistol. It moves along via rails automatically during the recoil process. The slide is also responsible for chambering ammunition and also extracting a spent casing from the chamber. It also moves as part of the recoil process and provides a link between the barrel and the closed-off portion of the back of the gun known as the breechblock.

Magazine: The magazine is what holds all the ammunition that the semiautomatic or machine pistol will fire, it is typically located in the gun's handle.

Machine pistols: A machine pistol is a handgun-style self-loading firearm that is magazine-fed and capable of both burst fire or fully automatic fire of pistol cartridges. While the line between machine pistols and compact submachine guns can be somewhat fluid, the term machine pistol typically refers to weapons that are a step up from the traditional semi-automatic pistol design through the use of modified fire control groups and typically include a modified disconnector and selector which are used to differentiate between semi-automatic and fully automatic fire.

As a small and easily concealable gun with a rapid rate of fire, these types of pistols see regular use in numerous different scenarios. Professional bodyguards often use them to guard high-profile VIPs and tactical police units often use them when they are operating in tight spaces. Furthermore, many militaries issue some form of machine pistol to soldier in instances of close-quarters combat.

Machine pistols and semiautomatic pistols work through the following process. First, the cartridge is fed into the chamber which moves the cartridge from the magazine and into the barrel. Once it reaches its destination, the gun is said to be chambered which means the cartridge has been fully added to the chamber. The next step is locking in which the slide and the barrel lock together. Once it has been locked, the next step is to fire the cartridge. The primer is hit by the firing pin, pressure builds in the gun and once enough has built up, it causes the bullet to leave the barrel.

Once the gun has been fired, the slide and the barrel then unlock and separate slightly. Extraction comes next as the slide moves backwards and the extractor hook pulls the empty casing of the spent cartridge out of the barrel by its rim. The ejector then hits the empty cartridge rim pushing it and turning out of the slide ejection port. Finally, the gun is cocked again which resets the action. This occurs as the firing pin and trigger are set together to allow another round to be fired if needed.

CHAPTER 3
Trigger Management and Hand Positioning

P rior to practicing with handguns in any capacity it is important to keep several different things in mind at all times. First, you will want to always assume that any gun you come into contact with is loaded which means you are always going to want to ensure that it is pointed in a safe direction. If you are practicing at a range then the safe direction is always going to be down range, away from other individuals. Even if the magazine is not currently in the gun and the slide is pulled back, it is always better to assume the gun is loaded.

Second, you are always going to want to make sure the gun is clear through the process of removing the magazine and setting it down away from the gun. With this done you will then want to rack the slide by moving it forward and backward a few times to guarantee that there is no round currently in the chamber. From there you will want to lock the slide in the back position so that the ejection port is clear in such a way that you can see any light shining through, guaranteeing that it is empty. With this done you will want to remove all of the rounds from the magazine before putting it back in the gun and pushing the slide forward. Once this is done your gun is ready to dry fire. Even with this done, it is important to visually inspect your practice target as well as what is behind it, just to be safe.

31

Hand positioning

Dominant hand grip: In general, the most effective type of shooting will be done with both hands on the grip whenever possible. This is the case because a two-handed grip will naturally lend more stability to the process which will improve your accuracy as well.

To accomplish this grip, you will want to hold the grip of the gun in your dominant hand near the top of the grip so the webbing between your thumb and index finger sits just below the slide. This will ensure that you have the greatest overall level of security when firing. You will then want to wrap your remaining fingers around the base of the grip directly below the trigger guard. You will want to keep them as close together as possible without overlapping. You will want to hold firmly, without succumbing to a death grip.

You will want to keep the index finger of your dominant hand extend directly against the frame of the gun and your shooting finger should be near the trigger but not on it unless you intend to fire. The thumb should be wrapped around the far side of the gun and pressed near the grip, touching the frame.

You will then want to add your non-dominant hand by placing it on the remaining exposed portion of the grip so that it covers it completely. The thumb of your non-dominant hand should be placed below and slightly in front of the thumb of your dominant hand and also pressed against the frame. With this done you will want to wrap your fingers around the base of the grip just underneath the trigger guard and also surrounding your dominant hand on the opposite side of the grip. Again, you will want to grip firmly without resorting to a death grip.

It is perfectly natural for this grip to feel awkward at first, much like holding a golf club correctly for the first time. The key to success is to fill the open space of the grip as completely as possible in order to mitigate as much recoil as you can. This will allow you to retain control of the gun after shooting and improve your accuracy over multiple shots. When you look down at the top of the gun when utilizing a proper hold both side should mirror one another.

Revolver thumb placement: If you are shooting a revolver then the ideal placement of your thumbs is going to differ from shooting a semiautomatic pistol. In this instance, you will want to use your nondominant hand's thumb to anchor your dominant hand by placing it on top of the back of your dominant hand and folding the distal knucklers over one another. Alternately you can rest the thumb of your support hand in the space between your dominant hand's thumb and forefinger. This option reduces overall recoil control, however and if you make the mistake of using it while firing a semiautomatic pistol it will leave your hand both pained and bloody.

Mistakes to avoid

Placing the strong finger on the trigger guard: Many new shooters make the mistake of placing their non-shooting index finger directly in front of the finger guard. This can cause a safety issue in stressful situations as during stressful situations this finger can easily drift inside the finger guard. This can easily cause an unintended discharge of the weapon if you are not careful and should be avoided at all costs.

Teacup hold: A teacup hold is when you cup your nondominant hand around the base of the grip, leaving one side of the gun unsupported. While this is the hold that is most commonly seen in movies and on television, in reality it will leave you with compromised control against recoil. While holding the base of the grip might be an extreme example, any lowering of the index finger on the support hand away from the side of the gun will start to decrease your ability to compensate for recoil. This type of hold can also naturally occur over time as the correct hold will naturally be tiring on your nondominant hand to start. This will ease over time, however, and it is important to not develop negative habits in the interim.

Using nondominant hand to support your wrist: This is another hold that is favored by the media but in reality, it is going to do little to either help your accuracy or to stabilize against recoil. Unless you are supporting a wrist that has recently been broken, there is no reason to attempt this hold.

Oddly sized gun: While it might seem awkward to hold a gun that seems too large for your hands at first, in reality there is virtually no gun that will be too large for you to handle effectively with practice. If you run across this situation, simply stick to the proper grip and practice, practice, practice. If you run across a gun that seems too small to handle comfortabley, that is if the little finger of your dominant hand hangs below the grip, then this can be mitigated by simply sliding your hand downward so the finger isn't the only part of your hand that hangs off the grip.

Trigger management

An accurate shot requires that the trigger be activated without moving the gun off the target. While this may sound simple, in reality it can be harder than it seems, especially when you take into account the recoil that will come with shooting the gun in a live fire scenario. The best way to ingrain in yourself what a successful trigger pull feels like is to simply practice dry firing your gun each and every day for approximately 10 minutes.

During this period, you are going to want to aim for a minimum of 25 clean trigger pulls. This will help you to develop the muscle memory required to feel what a perfect trigger pull feels like. Perfect trigger pulls are the key here, which means that if you slip up then that doesn't count as one of the 25, while this will mean you are pulling the trigger much more than 25 times to start, it will naturally improve with practice which is, after all, the point. A perfect trigger pull means that you have pressed the trigger straight to the rear and the front sight of the gun hasn't moved at all. If the front sight moves to the side or dips slightly then this is not a perfect trigger pull.

Wall drills: The wall drill was developed by a marksman named George Harris and is widely considered one of the most effective means of improving your marksmanship fundamentals. As with any dry fire drill, it bears repeating here that you always take the proper precautions before starting to practice which means following the cardinal rules of dry firing outlined at the start of this chapter.

Once you have checked and double-checked that your weapon is cleared you will want to find a nearby wall that will serve as a backstop in case an accident occurs. The wall you choose should be blank to ensure it provides no distractions and give you nothing really to aim at during the drill. This will allow you to focus all of your energy on your front sight to the exclusion of all else.

With this done, you will want to hold your unloaded weapon in a standard shooting grip and take the traditional stance (outlined in the next chapter) before pressing the muzzle of the gun to the wall so that it barely makes contact. You will then want to back off approximately one inch. From this position, you will want to practice proper trigger manipulation. Your goal should be to press the trigger straight back smoothly with a steady amount of pressure until the shot occurs without changing the alignment of your shot throughout the entire process. The key to accuracy here is a trigger press that doesn't interfere in any way with your sight picture.

If you find that your sight moves around as the trigger breaks, the first thing you are going to want to do is to slow down and give extra attention to your finger movement as well as your grip. Additionally, you will want to be aware if you are putting extra pressure on the grip with some of your other fingers. Another common issue is pressing the trigger with too much force which can cause additional movement at the last moment. Overall you will want to focus on keeping everything completely still except for the one finger that is pulling the trigger in a relaxed, smooth and slow trigger press.

If you are using a standard double action gun with the option for both single and double pulls then you will want to practice each as well. If you practice every day you should start seeing noticeable results within 30 to 45 days. If, after you have practiced for a month or so you still see variance when you practice at the range with live ammunition then take note of what type of movement you are seeing on the target and head back to the wall for additional practice, keeping in mind your range habits as you do so.

CHAPTER 4
Proper Stances

When it comes to shooting safely and accurately, stance is a crucial element of the process that is often overlooked by those who are just learning the fundamentals. In reality, however, a good stance is the foundation of your successful shooting platform. It may help to think of shooting in terms of building a house; no matter how well the upper stories are constructed, if the foundation is weak or flawed then the rest of the house will suffer.

When it comes to accurately shooting a handgun, regardless of the quality of your sight alignment, breath control and overall skills, if the stance you use doesn't provide you with a quality shooting platform then you will forever be an inconsistent shooter. When it comes to shooting accurately, consistency is the key to success which means stance is fundamental in order to shoot correctly when it really counts.

The different shooting stances that are frequently taught are outlined below, give each a try and see which one leaves you feeling the most stable overall.

Isosceles stance

While the Weaver stance has gained popularity in recent years, the isosceles stance was the primary stance taught to new shooters for decades. To use it properly, set your feet at shoulder width (or slightly more than shoulder width) apart from one another. The toes of your feet should face the target and align with each other in a parallel fashion. You will then flex your knees at an angle that will vary as you lean forward at the waist, bending slightly towards the target. You will then extend your arms so they form an isosceles triangle which is where this stance gets its name.

If you are still having problems with recoil, you can improve this somewhat by leaning farther forward when using this stance. To do so effectively you are going to want to place your shoulders forward from your hips, place your support-side foot forward slightly and bend your knees. Doing so will shift your posture and move your center of mass forward to ensure you have better control over the resulting recoil from firing your weapon.

Pros: The pros of this stance include the fact that it is a comfortable and natural position for most people to use when shooting. The position of the body also helps to improve the accuracy of many shooters.

Cons: The biggest downside to this stance is that while it increases stability of shooters who tend to move side to side, it does not provide much stability in the way of front to back balance as the position of the feet leave the shooter vulnerable in that capacity.

Weaver stance

The Weaver stance was first developed in the late 1950s by noted marksman Jack Weaver a deputy sheriff and range officer for the Los Angeles County Sheriff's office. During this period, Weaver was competing in quick draw, one on one shooting competitions where each shooter tried to pop a series of 12 balloons that were set up 21 feet from the firing line. The first person to pop all of the balloons won. Weaver developed his namesake technique as a way to draw his gun to eye level as quickly as possible while still ensuring that he could accurately aim from the sights and quickly developed a reputation for his speed and accuracy.

The Weaver stance is currently the most popular shooting stance being taught to new shooters these days. To use it, you start by placing your dominant foot back and turning to support the side of the body that is turned to face the target. You will then want to extend the arm on your firing side with the elbow of the nondominant hand bent in slightly. This will allow you to employ a combination push-pull grip that is exceedingly stable. Finally, you will want to push with your firing arm and pull with your support arm in order to stabilize the weapon.

The Weaver stance can also be modified in what is known as the Chapman stance. The general stance is going to be the same except that you fully extend your arms as if you were holding a rifle stock. Consistency is typically increased in this stance as your arm doesn't have to hover in the air as with the isosceles stance or the Weaver stance. It also improves recoil management as the dominant arm is fully extended. It is also useful for those who are cross-eyed as the opposite eye is going to naturally line up more easily with the line of the firearm. It is important to keep in mind that this variation of the stance can also put extra strain on the neck muscles.

Pros: This stance enhances front to back stability and the push and pull grip helps to control recoil significantly.

Cons: Turning the body in this fashion tends to leave an area of the body exposed in such a way that it makes a promising target for those who may be shooting back at you. If you are right-handed you will be exposing your left armpit which is a direct entry point to the heart. An additional problem with this stance is that moving while maintaining it can be difficult. Finally, many individuals who use this stance in practice ultimately resort to the isosceles stance when they have to use their weapon in an emergency.

Fighting stance: This stance is also known as the modified isosceles or modified Weaver stance. This stance was developed for military uses in the special forces community. It has since become popular among law enforcement due to the ability of those using it to easily defend themselves with their hands or firearm without having to switch out of it. While more of an advanced technique, it is useful for civilian shooters as well due to its ability to naturally square the target.

To utilize this stance, you are going to want to stand with your feet shoulder width apart with your firing foot slightly behind your support foot. Ideally you will want to position yourself so that the toe of your shooting foot is at the instep of your support foot. This offset stance will eliminate the front to back balance issue of the standard isosceles stance. You will also want to flex your needs in order to absorb any extra recoil and also to act as a form of shock absorption when moving in a given direction. You will also want to lean forward slightly and to extend your arms straight out while bringing the sight up to eye level. You will want to keep your head level and maintain your balance, especially while moving.

Pros: This stance is useful when firing any weapon, not just a handgun.

Cons: This stance has no real downsides as it modifies both the Weaver and the isosceles stance in such a way that it removes their drawbacks.

49

TIM L. GARDNER.

CHAPTER 5
Draw and Reload Efficiently

Drawing a gun efficiently

Many amateur shooters don't believe that they need to be that quick on the draw as they aren't law enforcement or military and thus won't have to worry about getting into a shootout scenario. This is faulty thinking however, as drawing your gun without clear cause in most situations will cause a stir among those in your general vicinity and can lead to a whole host of additional issue on its own. As such, the average civilian is more likely to need to draw their weapon only once a clear threat has been identified which means that without being quick on the draw you may be too late.

Additionally, it is important to keep in mind that if you find yourself in need of drawing your gun for a serious purpose, your best draw is likely to become your worst draw. As such, if your best draw is above average, then your draw in combat is likely to be average and if your best draw is below average to start then you may end up getting your gun stuck in your holster, or worse, when the time comes to do so in a real-world scenario. As such, the more practice you can get, the better.

Drawing properly

While it might seem innocuous at first, the drawing of your weapon from its holster is one of the most potentially dangerous things you can do when it comes to handling a gun. Safety and speed are on the other ends of the spectrum which means that it is important to keep the following in mind in order to stay safe and shoot accurately.

The most common way of drawing a gun has it traveling from the holster the shooting position in a diagonal, straight upward motion. There are two major problems with this type of draw. First, the gun is not generally in a good firing position until the arm is fully extended which means that even up close the threat cannot be engaged effectively very quickly. Second, if you find yourself in a confined space then the gun is often going to hit an object and ruin your draw.

Right angle draw stroke: The right angle draw stroke has been gaining popularity for the past twenty years or so and it solves both of these problems. Also known as the close quarters draw, this draw has the gun angling towards the target as soon as it clears the holster. To do so you are going to want to draw up along the side of your chest, following the ribcage to where it meets the support hand. You will then want to extend towards the target as needed. This leaves you with a clear opening to fire as soon as possible.

The right-angle draw is more effective than a standard draw because it allows you to determine the right time to draw without all the wasted time spent getting into position first. It is also more likely to clear nearby object as it is tucked into the chest prior to the extension.

Draw stroke: The first action in the draw stroke should actually be a combination of three different actions that you will need to practice in order to ensure that they happen practically instantaneously. First, your body will need to shift into a combat position by moving your nondominant leg forward and slightly outward while at the same time leaning forward slightly in order to distribute your wait to help with recoil. Second, you support hand will want to move up towards your chest in order to get it out of the way of stray bullets. This will also make it easier to move into a more traditional stance when you are ready to do so.

Finally, you are going to need to have the correct grip on the pistol. This is extremely important as having even a passable handle on the grip has the potential to end poorly which means you are going to want to regrip if you feel your initial grip is subpar. Regripping after the draw means you are going to need to worry about changing hand position when you should be worried about shooting accurately and is not recommended.

Once you have these things out of the way you will want to lift, then meet and finally extend. You will want to lift your gun straight out of the holster, and, once it has cleared angle it upwards facing the target. You will then want to move it up and over before extending it into your line of vision facing the target.

Tips for drawing effectively in a real-life scenario

Keep the right posture: Starting from a crouching position will naturally give you a more confident grip while also improving accuracy and reducing recoil. It will also help to reduce your overall profile which means you will be less of a target if anyone is coming after you. Finally, it makes it easier to shoot while moving while still retaining accuracy.

Be sure to move: Standing still while drawing your gun naturally makes you a more obvious target. Moving while drawing can take some practice but it can also save your life in a life-or-death situation. Find a range where you can practice moving even a few feet, when the time comes to practice what you have learned, you will be glad you did.

Point the gun in the right direction: Make a point of practicing drawing your gun and immediately pointing it at a target. This way, if the time comes, you will be able to fire once from the hip before you can fire again when the gun reaches chest level and then fire a third time once you have gotten into the appropriate stance. When practicing this technique, it is important to keep your nondominant hand close to your chest to avoid accidentally shooting yourself in the process. This is especially true if you favor the Weaver stance so it is worth practicing in case the worst happens.

Only place your finger on the trigger if you are going to fire: If you keep your finger on the trigger then you essentially remove the option not to fire. Especially if you are in a combat scenario, it is natural for your trigger finger to be moving around more than normal. What's more, studies show that it is just as quick to move your finger from the appropriate position and fire as it is to fire from directly on the trigger, so you aren't saving any time and only increasing your overall risk. Avoid accidental discharge from an itchy trigger finger, only put your finger on the trigger if you plan to pull it.

Be sure to practice drawing without firing: Muscle memory is a powerful thing which means that if all you ever practice is drawing and firing then whenever you draw your gun you are going to be tempted to fire it without consciously making the decision to do so. It doesn't take an expert marksman to see why this is a bad idea. To counter this type of muscle memory practice drawing without firing just as often as you practice drawing and firing.

Reloading properly

Semiautomatic and machine pistol reloading:
First and foremost, even if you think your gun is empty, it is important to still treat it as though it is loaded. If your semiautomatic pistol is empty then the slide will typically lock back into place once the final shot has been fired. You should also be able to see the empty chamber clearly through the ejection port. If the slide has not locked then it is likely there is still a round in the chamber.

To reload properly, take the thumb of your dominant hand and press the button for the magazine release which can typically be found on the grip near the trigger. Some magazines will drop out of the grip automatically and some will need to be pulled free, it all depends on the model of gun you are using.

Next, you will want to pick up the loaded magazine by the front edge, which you can feel by the fact that it is the narrower side of the magazine. It is also the side which the bullets are facing. You will then want to push the magazine into the gun by placing the back side of the magazine firmly against the back of the space where it will go (known as the magazine well) You will then want to push upward firmly until you hear it click.

Once it has clicked, you will want to pull downward on the magazine to ensure that it is properly in place and fully seated. This step is extremely important as failing to ensure the magazine is seated is the leading cause of malfunction with this type of pistol. One you are sure the magazine is seated properly you will then want to place your nondominant hand on the top of the slide, grasp it firmly and pull back sharply until it stops sliding. Once you release the slide it will naturally snap forward and cause the first round to automatically chamber if you did everything properly. This sliding motion is important so you will want to avoid holding onto the slide as it moves into place, nor will you want to attempt to ease it down slowly.

Revolver: To correctly load a revolver, the first thing you are going to want to do is to open the loading gate found on the right side of the gun. Make sure you center the chamber in the loading gate before loading the first bullet. Next you will want to rotate the cylinder so that it moves past the second cylinder and on to the third. You will then want to load the remaining cylinders. Once you have loaded all of the chambers in the cylinder you will want to point the gun in a safe direction and bring the hammer to full cock. Assuming you have done things correctly the hammer will come down on the unloaded chamber. It is important to leave a chamber unloaded in older guns as a hard blow to the gun can cause a misfire. The same can occur if you make a mistake while bringing the hammer down.

The most common issue that comes along with loading a revolver is getting the fresh cartridges to drop properly into the chamber. If even a single cartridge is peeking out then the cylinder won't close and you will have to deal with the issue before firing. The easiest way to ensure that this won't be the case is by keeping the revolver clean. The chamber can easily become fouled when firing and if you don't clean it regularly you will have problems loading and unloading.

CHAPTER 6
Malfunction Troubleshooting Techniques

As with any other type of machinery, handguns can experience malfunctions. Unlike many types of machinery, not being able to handle these malfunctions properly can lead to serious injury in addition to damaging the handgun, possibly beyond repair. Below are the most common types of malfunctions and how to clear them. As always, check and double check that your gun is unloaded before attempting any of them.

Hang fire: If you pull the trigger and your gun doesn't fire, the most likely reason is what is known as a hang fire scenario. A hang fire is caused when there is a delay with the propellant being ignited in the projectile. If you believe this malfunction is occurring them the first thing you are going to want to do is to keep the gun pointed downrange for at least 1 minute. This will insure that the propellant isn't actually going to ignite and give you a scare, or worse. Once this time has elapsed you are going to want to clear the dud from the gun and place it into water to ensure it isn't still going to go off.

Squib load: A squib load is one of the most dangerous types of malfunctions you can encounter. It takes place when a bullet fails to generate enough force to properly exit the barrel and instead gets lodged there. If this happens and you don't notice before firing another round the second round will run into the first which will cause the barrel to bulge (at best) or explode (at worst). Needless to say, this can lead to extreme injury or even death. If you are perceptive, you can always tell when a squib load has occurred because it sounds different than a traditional shot. Specifically, it will be much quieter or even muffled completely.

If you fire a shot and it doesn't sound quite right, you will want to start by clearing your pistol and then checking the barrel for obstructions. It is important to never look down the barrel if you expect a squib load and to instead find something that will not scratch the barrel, a pencil for example, and place it inside the barrel to make sure that it is clear.

A squib load is typically caused by a round that has primer but not enough powder. A round that has typically been reloaded is the most likely reason that this type of malfunction occurs.

Failure to feed: A failure to feed malfunction occurs when the next round in a magazine fails to load into the firing chamber properly. There are many different reasons that this can occur, including that the magazine was not loaded properly. A failure to feed malfunction will typically prevent the slide of your pistol from moving forward properly as the cartridge has not traveled the full distance required to become chambered. Once you remove the magazine, the offending round will most likely drop down into the magazine well after the slide has been locked back.

Stovepipe: A stovepipe malfunction typically occurs when a spent cartridge doesn't eject properly which can cause it to become lodged in the ejection port. This type of malfunction most typically occurs if you are not holding your weapon correctly. Locking the slide back with typically clear the blockage.

Slide lock malfunction: When everything is working as it should, a tab that is located near the top left side of the magazine follower connects to the slide lock and protrudes into the interior of the frame. When the last round is taken from a magazine, the follower then moves into the topmost position. After this last round is ejected, the follower then pushes the slide lock up and into a small space that is cut out of the slide, locking it into the rear position in the process.

When the process doesn't work as it should, the slide can move up to engage the slide while there are still cartridges in the magazine. Nearly all modern pistols have an internal spring that is connected to the slide stop assembly which makes it difficult for this movement to take place. Alternately, there may be an external spring and plunger that are used to generate friction against the slide stop to prevent accidental misfires. A malfunction can occur if the slide stop is weak or damaged or if the plunger spring needs to be replaced. It can also occur if the magazine is damaged or if it is not the exact right magazine for the firearm you are using.

While this malfunction can be caused by wear and tear to the weapon, the primary cause is typically caused by the shooter accidentally grazing the slide stop and moving it upward during the gun's recoil. If you run into this malfunction the first thing you will want to do is to ensure that you were not the cause. You will then want to check the magazine to ensure proper contact was maintained with the slide stop. If that is not the cause then you will want to check the components to ensure there is no undue wear and tear.

Cartridge fails to strip from the magazine: This type of malfunction can occur when a round is fired and the case extracts and ejects properly but the next round is not stripped from the magazine which allows the slide to move forward and lock onto an empty chamber. The biggest cause of this issue is if the magazine is not properly seated. To ensure this doesn't happen to you, it is best to always check that not only is there a round in the chamber but that the magazine is insert correctly before you begin shooting. Generally, you will be able to correct this problem by simply giving the bottom of the magazine a firm tap, followed by racking the slide again.

If this doesn't solve the problem then you will need to consider potential problems within the mechanical interactions in the pistol. There is a small space in the magazine that contacts with the internal surface of the catch which locks the magazine into its predetermined spot in the frame. If the magazine is damaged or if the gun is dirty and there is debris or dirt blocking this space then the magazine may not fully seat. This can cause the slide to skip over the next cartridge in the magazine and cause this malfunction.

Nose down chamber feed failure: This type of malfunction can occur when the tip of a cartridge connects with the feed ramp on a downward angle which causes it to not feed into the chamber correctly and halt the motion of the slide in the process causing the pistol to jam. This can be caused by several different things including a malfunction in the cartridge, feed ramp, extractor or the magazine.

First you will want to check to ensure that the magazine has been seated properly as otherwise the slide may be skipping. This can also occur when the magazine is seated low enough that the slide doesn't even catch the base of the cartridge. If this is the case or if the follower isn't pushing the cartridge to the required height the breech face of the slide may contact only the top side of the cartridge base which can then cause the rim of the case to move underneath the extractor as it moves up the breech face. Alternately, it can cause the cartridge's forward movement to move in a downward angle.

The issue may also be with the extractor. In this case when the slide moves forward and the breech face comes into contact with the next cartridge then the base of the cartridge will move up the breech face, ensuring the primer is positioned in front of the firing pin where it needs to be and is then held in place by the extractor. If there is too much or too little tension in the extractor then it can prevent the case from aligning properly within the chamber as it is pulled from the magazine.

The problem could also be caused by the feed ramp and the cartridge itself. When it comes to the feed ramp, the barrel can be crafted in one of two ways. It can be ramped with the feed ramp being incorporated into the design of the barrel or it can be part of the frame instead. If the feed ramp has been corroded or damaged, or if there is a misalignment or seem in a two-part design then this can cause enough friction when the cartridge contacts the freed ramp to stop forward momentum.

Finally, the issue may be in the design of the cartridge itself. If the cartridge is blunt and short, then it can be more likely to end up nose down when fed. This is caused by the increased distance between the tip of the projectile and the feed ramp as well as the shape of the surface that will connect with the feed ramp. Rounded projectiles and longer cartridges both tend to feed more easily without experiencing this problem.

If you find yourself experiencing this type of malfunction then you are going to want to start by checking your cartridges, feed ramp, extractor tension and magazine and make sure they are all in working order. In many cases keeping these elements clean is enough to eliminate the problem

CHAPTER 7
Moving Targets and Multiple Targets

Moving targets

While practicing against a stationary target is a great way to improve your accuracy, if you ever find yourself in an actual confrontation where you need to shoot at another person it is important to keep in mind that once the bullets start flying, your targets are going to start moving. As such, it is important to learn how to hit a moving target if you are going to be able to effectively protect yourself and your loved ones in real-world scenarios.

In order to effectively hit moving targets with a handgun, it is important to keep in mind a handful of relevant principles. First and foremost, if you have ever shot flying targets you need to forget everything you learned as it will not help you in this instance. Flying targets tend to move much faster than ground-based targets which means the lead times are going to be much shorter when shooting at them.

Second, the reason a majority of defensive marksmen miss moving targets is that they stop the swing of their pistol the moment the gun fires. Unfortunately for them, this results in the bullet moving past the intended target without hitting them. This is caused by a chain of events that starts when your brain makes the decision to fire. Once this action occurs it takes a few moments for your hand to respond which means the shot doesn't take place instantaneously. Instead, first the impulse to fire has to move down your spinal cord to the brachial nerve before moving to your finger, then your trigger finger needs to contract around the trigger.

Once the trigger has been pulled then the primer needs to be struck and detonator which will cause the powder to ignite. Then the powder needs to cause a buildup of pressure so the bullet can be released from the cartridge. Then the bullet needs to move down the barrel and then it must travel the distance to the target. What all of this means is that if you stop moving your gun when your brain thinks fire, your bullet will hit the point where the target was a handful of microseconds after they have moved from that point.

To determine how much you need to continue moving your gun in order to hit a moving target after you have made the decision to fire, the best option is to utilize what are known as runners which can be found at most larger shooting ranges. A runner is a moving target that moves along a track or a set of wires that is perfect for your needs in this scenario.

If you do not currently have access to this type of training, the next best thing is to simply keep the gun moving while tracking the target in your sites and work the trigger in a smooth a repetitive fashion. You can practice this type of action by setting up multiple targets next to one another so that they are spread out about three or four yards from one another. You will then want to fire a single round at each target, working your way from one side to the other so that they are all engaged in a continuous swing. The shots you take should have practically no time in between them. So, instead of 1...2...3 it should be 1,2,3. Another way to think about this is that all four shots should sound as if they are being shot at a single stationary target in a four-shot string.

You will want to shoot from right to left and then do another pass that is left to right. Once you have mastered this transition and can do it smoothly, you will want to move on to firing two shots at each target. You will want to keep this up until the shots are completely consecutive and sound like a single eight-shot string.

What you will be learning here is to track the front sight as the gun is on the move. When the front sight begins to rise due to recoil, you will want to learn to automatically bring it back in line without even consciously thinking about it. This correction should happen as it occurs rather than at the end of the cycle.

If you keep up with this practice regiment at a variety of standard pistol engagement distances then it will be difficult for anyone to move fast enough on foot to keep out of your spray of gunfire unless they are running at a flat out sprint which means they are unlikely to pose much of a threat to you anyway.

Multiple targets

One situation that all defensive-minded shooters need to be prepared for is a scenario where there are multiple targets converging on you all at once.

Efficient transitions: One of the primary challenges you will need to consider when it comes to dealing with multiple targets is the natural inclination to get ahead of yourself. If you are thinking about the second target before you finish dealing with the first then you are more likely to miss your first target, throwing your entire plan into disarray. This means you are going to want to keep your sights on the first target for long enough to ensure a hit before moving onto the next.

When you do get to move onto the next target it is important to move your weapon as efficiently as possible. Many marksmen do so by moving their upper body in the same fashion as the turret of a tank, keeping their eyes on the sights as the weapon moves to the next target. There are a few things not in your favor about this strategy, however, the first of which is your reaction time. As the sights move between targets it takes additional time for your eyes to inform your brain that it is time to stop the pistol before your brain has to tell your hands the same thing. This means it is surprisingly easy to overshoot your target when using this method. Inertia also contributes to this problem as once you get your weapon in motion it can take precious extra seconds to bring it to a stop.

Rather, a more efficient means of transitioning between targets is to move your eyes and then your weapon. Once your eyes have established where you want your pistol to point, you can then move your weapon to the desired spot without having to worry about inertia working against you. Your head will remain in the same position and your body will bring the sight up to your eyes without ever taking your eye off the intended target. This can be effective with both target-focused shooting and precision-sighted shooting.

Prioritize greatest threats: In addition to transitioning between targets as effectively as possible, it is also important to prioritize the targets you want to take out so that you deal with the most pressing threat first. Once this threat has been dealt with you move onto the greatest remaining threat and so on and so forth. A common example of this is two enemies, one with a pistol and one with a shotgun. While the shotgun wielding enemy is naturally going to be the most dangerous of the two, all things being equal, there is more to determine about the situation as well. For example, you would also need to take into account the distance of the two attackers as the shotgun wielding attacker will not be as great of a threat as the individual with the pistol until he is at a closer range.

Spread fire: This is an alternate method of multiple-target engagement where all of the potential threats are considered to have equal priority. This type of engagement can be useful if you won't be able to mitigate the danger from each of the targets before they are able to get in range to potentially threaten your life. As such, instead of focusing on individuals and giving the others a chance to attack you as well you would want to take shots at each one of them in turn with one shot each, spreading the damage that you can do around and thus preventing any of them from doing anything seriously harmful in the interim.

In order to see why this method is effective, it is important to keep in mind that a gunshot wound is not an all or nothing proposition. While it may be your natural inclination to deal with one target completely, for example by expending three shots to ensure they will no longer be a threat, in reality one shot, even if you just manage to hit them in the arm, is going to be enough to dramatically hinder their effectiveness long enough so that you can do the same to the other attackers.

CHAPTER 8
Practical Drills to Perfect Marksmanship Fundamentals

Trigger control

Trigger control is of key importance when it comes to perfecting your fundamentals as it is a major point of improving your accuracy. This is because, while the pistol is a naturally accurate weapon, few untrained individuals handle it in a way that promotes accuracy. Luckily, there are drills that can change that.

Brass on the front sight: This drill is easier to complete with the help of a partner. First you will want to start by ensuring your weapon is ready to dry fire. Start by resetting the action

84

on your pistol before getting your partner to balance a piece of brass that has been spent on the front sight. Next, you will want to execute a clean, smooth press on the trigger. You will know you have done this correctly if you can complete the move without the brass falling to the ground. If the brass hits the ground then you will know that you are jerking the trigger and causing your gun to move unnecessarily. The secret to keeping the brass where it is placed is a continuous trigger press with a clean break once you are finished.

Let the slack out: The greater the amount the trigger moves, the greater the probability that you will miss your shot. Each trigger press is really made up of three distinct stages. The first is the slop which is the name given to the distance the trigger will need to travel in order to meet resistance. The second is the slack which is the name for the amount of distance the trigger will travel under pressure prior to causing the weapon to fire. The third is the shot which is where the trigger will finish its movement and cause the gun to fire. With each press of the trigger you will move through all three stages practically without thinking about them. However, with additional shots fired, the trigger does not reset to zero. Instead, the distance required for reset will only be as far as the slack. Keep this in mind and don't release the trigger more than is required.

A useful drill to get into this habit is to prepare your gun for dry firing and then press the trigger. Using your nondominant hand, you will want to rack the slide and then, as it is moving forward, relax your trigger finger completely. The tension in the trigger will move it forward, generating a reset. When this occurs, you are only going to want to allow the trigger to move forward the bare minimum amount. A steady stream of practice will allow you to build muscle memory around how far your trigger will need to travel in order to hit the reset point. Letting the trigger move further than this will result in a slap of the trigger when it is pulled which tends to interfere with accuracy.

Follow through

Follow through applies to remaining steady enough between shots to ensure that each shot hits its target. Many individuals have issues with this due to anticipation which causes them to flinch which is especially common among new marksman. The following drills can help mitigate these issues.

Ball and dummy: This is a drill that is great when it comes to eliminating flinch and is typically most effective when done with a partner. To start, you turn away from your weapon and have your partner set the pistol either with a live round in the chamber or not. You then turn back around and attempt to fire the weapon down range, if your muzzle dips then this is a sign that you are anticipating the shot. The split between live and dry firing should be about 25/75 with the majority of shots being dry fires. With enough practice the anticipation of firing a live round will be cured and your shots will be more accurate as a result.

Single shot drill: This drill is also effective when it comes to mitigating the loss of accuracy that can come from anticipating a shot. This is an easy to handle drill that can be practiced solo. To start, you will want to load a single round into the chamber and then remove the magazine from the weapon. Aim down range and shoot the live round before shooting again with the empty weapon. Be prepared for your self-diagnosis and keep an eye out for signs of dipping as this means you are still anticipating the shot.

Alignment and Sight Picture

At the most reliable and fundamental level, the function of the sights is to align your shot on the target through the use of the front sight. When done correctly, the target and the rear sights are going to be somewhat blurry while the front sight is crystal clear. The following drills will help to build confidence with this practice.

Bench shooting: One of the most effective ways to master specific aspects of shooting is to reduce the amount of focus that is required for the other aspects. In this case, shooting from a sitting position will mean that you don't need to worry about proper stabilization in order to shoot reliably. This type of practice will not only help you to increase your confidence, it will help to improve your alignment sight habits as well. To practice this technique all you need to do is to sit on a bench and rest your arms on a shooting bag. Take your time between shots and keep in mind your goal is to manage perfect sights throughout the training. Focus on gaining better alignment and always acquire a sight picture that is reliable.

Figure eight drill: If you feel as though your sights tend to shift when you make a shot, it is important to keep in mind that this is frequently a perception issue and does not reflect reality. If you have good mechanics then you should still make your shots consistently. The figure eight drill will help you to align your perception with reality. Start roughly six yards away from your target and point your pistol at it before taking the slack and slop off the trigger. With this done you will then want to move the sight between six and eight inches around the bullseye in a figure eight pattern. When you cross the bullseye, you will want to break the shot before resetting the trigger and shooting again. Repeat this process between six and eight times. Doing so will show you that you are really more accurate than you think and help to match your perceptions with reality.

Mixing techniques

While practicing individual techniques is useful, your end goal should always be to bring these components together as there are many moving pieces when it comes to making a successful shot. The following drills will do just that.

Ragged hole drill: To perform this drill you will want to set your target about six yards from where you are standing. You will then want to slowly fire five rounds into the target, aiming for the same point every time. During this exercise, you will want to focus on the smallest portion of the target possible. Ideally, you will want to use a target that has one or two-inch dots on it to use as focus points. While practicing, you will want to take your time and do your best to hit the exact same spot with each shot without having to try and make corrections or chase your shots. If you can manage your fundamentals correctly the end result should be one ragged hole. If your shots end up spread out then you know you need to practice your fundamentals more thoroughly.

Shrinking target drill: This exercise is broadly similar to the ragged hole drill. Here your goal is to focus on generating the smallest shot groupings possible. To start you will want to find a target that has several circles on it, each somewhat smaller than the last. Standing six yards away you are going to want to shoot five rounds into each circle. Your goals should be to get all of your shots into the circle. Once you master a circle then you can start to focus on the next smaller one and so on and so forth. This exercise will not only boost your skills, it will boost your confidence as well.

Draw single shot drill: This drill is great for bringing all the fundamentals together. You will want to start in a holstered position and then draw your weapon and fire towards the bullseye in one single motion before holstering your weapon once more. Repeat this ten times and then reset. Your goal here should be to shoot solid shots while also drawing. If your groups begin to widen then you will want to slow down. If you are already successfully shooting ragged holes then you will want to speed up instead.

CHAPTER 9
Alternative Shooting Techniques

Point shooting

P oint shooting is a way of shooting a pistol both quickly and accurately in a way that does not require you to use the sights in a life-threatening situation in close quarters where you have the greatest risk of personal injury. If you find yourself in a scenario where your life is being threatened by another individual who is holding a weapon then you will often have a difficult time utilizing standard marksmanship techniques. In order to prevent this scenario from costing you life and limb you will want to become so accustomed to your weapon that you can aim it without thinking about the action reliably enough to not need to focus on the sights in order to hit a nearby target.

While this might seem impossible at first, with enough practice you will find that you can establish a type of subconscious coordination between your brain, hands and eyes through the use of a little known human sense by the name of proprioception to make it easier to fire your weapon by instinct. Proprioception is the sense of the relative position of your body in relation to the world around you and the effort and strength that is required for specific movements. It is made possible by proprioceptors in the tendons and skeletal striated muscles as well as the fibrous capsules in the joints.

Proprioception is activated by proprioceptors in your peripheral vison. This sense is assumed to be comprised of information that is gathered from a combination of sensory neurons in the inner ear, of all places, as well as the stretch receptors located in the muscles and joint supporting ligaments. Additionally, it is thought to correspond with finger kinesthesia which is based around skin sensation and haptic perception. If you are looking to increase your proprioception skills even further, it is recommended that you take up juggling.

Aimed point shooting: The aimed point shooting method has been in use since the 1800s. To utilize this method, you simply ensure that your index finger is aligned with the side of your pistol while pulling the trigger with your middle finger. Then, without consciously aiming at your target you instead point in the direction you know them to be and let your body do the rest. This is especially effective if you are caught off guard and have to draw extremely quickly against an enemy that is rapidly moving in your direction. If you plan on using this method it is important that you aren't using a pistol that has a protruding slide stop as then the use of this method can result in the gun jamming.

The US Army Field Manual specifically recommends this type of shooting in close quarters noting "When a soldier points, he instinctively points at the feature on the object on which his eyes are focused. An impulse from the brain causes the arm and hand to stop when the finger reaches the proper position. When the eyes are shifted to a new object or feature, the finger, hand, and arm also shift to this point. It is this inherent trait that can be used by the soldier to rapidly and accurately engage targets."

Pistol quick kill: This method was popularized in the late 1990s by Robin Brown, a student of the famous marksman Lucky McDaniel. To utilize this method, you will want to grip your pistol and point it at the target in the same way you would point your finger if you were mimicking a gun with your hand. When forming a finger gun, there is no notion of sighting or aiming, you simply point your finger at what you are going to pantomime shooting. The end result is a trajectory that is somewhat below your peripheral vision, anywhere from between two and four inches underneath eye level.

When pointing a gun at a target in this fashion you are going to see the end of the barrel along with the top of the front sight as you look at the target. To perform this method properly you do not want to look at the gun or the front site at all, you will just want to simply look at the target. The benefit of this style of shooting is that you never need to take your eye off of the target which is useful if you are aiming at a hostile target who is likely to take any reduction of attention as an opportunity to move or to cause you physical harm.

Quick fire aimed: The quick fire method is another method that is taught by the US army. To utilize this method of firing you are going to want raise your weapon to average firing height and use your firing eye just above the back sighting aperture while using the front sight to draw a bead on the target. With proper practice, this method can be used to aim and fire in less than a single second with adequate accuracy up to 25 yards.

Quick fire pointed: If you have even less time available to you, you can also simply keep your weapon at your side and simply fire a single shot or multiple shots in a row. When doing so, you will want to keep both of your eyes open and rely on your natural instincts regarding peripheral vision to properly line up your weapon with your target. This method is considered useful and accurate up to 15 yards from the target.

Power point stance

While a two-handed stance is always going to be the most accurate, there are naturally going to be times when you aren't able to use both of your hands effectively to take the shot. The power point stance is useful in those scenarios as it allows you to deliver accurate and fast shots at close range using either your dominant or nondominant hand. This stance is naturally more aggressive than that which is used by those who compete in bullseye competitions, but the goal here isn't to strive for pinpoint accuracy, it is to get a shot off as quickly as possible while still retaining some reasonable degree of accuracy.

To get into this stance you will want to set your foot that corresponds to the hand you are holding the gun with between 15 and 20 inches ahead of your other foot. You will then want to push your shoulder into the gun and flex your knees. This is similar to the way that boxers stand when throwing a hard punch, you are essentially driving the gun into the target. You will then want to tuck your other hand tightly to the center of your chest, if possible. This will help to solidify the muscles of the upper shoulder and promote improved trigger control in the process.

Pros: This stance can be entered into quickly and provides relative accuracy despite only using one hand.

Cons: This stance provides less accuracy and stability than two-handed stances and, while it should be practiced, should only be used in scenarios where you don't have time to line up a two-handed stance.

Strong-hand retention stance

You may occasionally find yourself in scenarios where extending your gun means that it is likely to be taken away from you. If you find yourself in this type of scenario then the strong-hand retention stance may be extremely useful. To use this stance, you are going to want to hold the gun one-handed and keep the elbow tucked close to your body with your hand only a few inches ahead of your body. Your support hand will move to the support shoulder at about the same height in order to keep it clear of the muzzle and keep it ready to fend off a nearby attacker. This will ensure the gun is locked close to the body while at the same time leaving you a free hand to act as required. Foot placement isn't required with this stance as it is primarily used while moving.

If a threat does appear then all you need to do is to pivot your upper body in order to bring the gun to bear and fire. If the threat appears at a longer range then your support hand is ready to come into play as you shift to a more useful stance. There is a serious caveat with this stance, however, if you are using a gun with a ported barrel, or one that has a compensator then you will not want to use this stance as unburned powder or powder gasses will blow directly into your eyes and face if you do so. If this is the case then you will want to extend the gun to a safe distance while still retaining full control.

Pros: This stance allows for maximum gun control at close range.

Cons: This stance provides limited stability and proof against recoil, additionally it provides limited accuracy at long range.

CONCLUSION

Thank you for making it through to the end of *How to Shoot a Handgun: Handgun Marksmanship Fundamentals for Real Life Situations*, let's hope it was informative and able to provide you with all of the tools you need to achieve your goals, whatever it is that they may be. Just because you've finished this book doesn't mean there is nothing left to learn on the topic, expanding your horizons is the only way to find the mastery you seek. Additionally, it is important that you always treat your gun as if it were loaded and do everything in your power in order to ensure that your pistol usage is as safe as it can possibly be at all times and in all situations. Never forget that it only takes a few seconds of carelessness to cause irreversible harm.

While learning about these techniques and drills is a great way to familiarize yourself with the basics, it is important to keep in mind that the only way to ever truly be ready to prepare yourself to use a pistol in a real-life scenario is through practice, practice, practice. While at first, everything from assuming the proper stance to holding your pistol correctly may very well feel awkward, the feeling of awkwardness will fade in time. You have already gone ahead and purchased a weapon for self-protection, it only makes sense that you do everything in your power to ensure that you are able to use it effectively, and safely as possible should the need arise.

The more you practice on the range and with dry-fire scenarios, the less you will have to think about the fundamentals if the time comes and you have to use your weapon to protect yourself and your family. Remember, the difference between success and failure can be simply a matter of seconds and if you are in a life and death situation that small amount of time can make a big difference

Finally, if you found this book useful in anyway, a review on Amazon is always appreciated!

www.ingramcontent.com/pod-product-compliance
Lightning Source LLC
LaVergne TN
LVHW021537080426
835509LV00019B/2694